POINT OF IMPACT

The Cuban Missile Crisis

To the Brink of World War III

FERGUS FLEMING

Heinemann Library
Chicago, Illinois

Produced for Heinemann Library by Discovery Books Limited
Designed by Ian Winton
Illustrations by Stefan Chabluk
Printed in Hong Kong

05 04 03 02 01
10 9 8 7 6 5 4 3 2 1

Library of Congress Cataloging-in-Publication Data

Fleming, Fergus, 1959–
        The Cuban Missile Crisis : to the brink of World War III / Fergus Fleming.
            p. cm.— (Point of impact)
        Includes bibliographical references and index.
        ISBN 1-58810-075-8 (library binding)
            1. Cuban Missile Crisis, 1962—Juvenile literature. 2. World
politics—1955–1965—Juvenile literature. 3. World War III—Juvenile literature. [1. Cuban
Missile Crisis, 1962. 2. World politics—1955–1965.] I. Title. II. Series.

        E841 .F55 2001
        973.922—dc21

                                                                        00-046095

Acknowledgments
The Publishers would like to thank the following for permission to reproduce photographs:
Corbis, p. 24 and front cover (top); Corbis/Bettmann, pp. 12, 14, 16, 19, 22, 25 and front cover (bottom), 29;
Hulton Getty, pp. 4, 8, 10, 13, 15, 18, 20, 23, 28; Corbis/Hulton-Deutsch, pp. 5, 21; Popperfoto, pp. 7, 27;
Peter Newark's American Pictures, p. 11; Science Museum/Science and Society Picture Library, p. 11;
Corbis/Everett, p. 26.

Cover photographs reproduced with permission of Corbis and Corbis/Bettmann

Every effort has been made to contact copyright holders of any material reproduced in this book. Any omissions will be rectified in subsequent printings if notice is given to the Publisher.

Some words are shown in bold, **like this.** You can find out what they mean by looking in the glossary.

Contents

To the Brink of War

Soviet missiles on Cuba

For fourteen days in October 1962, the world stood on the brink of destruction. The **Soviet Union** had placed **nuclear missiles** on the Caribbean island of Cuba, just 90 miles (145 kilometers) off the Florida coast. The United States military was on full alert, poised to attack. In Cuba, meanwhile, Soviet commanders stood ready to fire their missiles if a U.S. invasion took place. Neither side was willing to back down. Unless an agreement was reached, the crisis could turn into a world war.

President Kennedy breaks the news that there are Soviet missiles in Cuba. His live television broadcast frightened the nation.

Threat and counterthreat

For such a small island, Cuba was very important. After a revolution, it had become the only **communist** nation in the Americas in 1959. The Soviet Union saw it as a point of entry into the Western Hemisphere. Intimidated by **NATO** missiles just across their borders, the Soviets believed that their missiles on Cuban soil would even things up. The United States, on the other hand, saw the Cuban missiles as a threat to its own security.

Neither the U.S. nor the Soviet Union seriously wanted to go to war. They were the two biggest nuclear powers on the globe, and they knew that if they used the weapons at their disposal the consequences would be catastrophic and might even lead to the end of human civilization. However, in the case of Cuba, it looked as if war might be the only option.

Too close for comfort

Global calamity was prevented at the last moment when U.S. President John F. Kennedy and Soviet Premier Nikita Khrushchev made a face-saving deal. Both sides declared they had come out best; but it was the United States that really won, having forced the Soviets to retreat at little cost to itself.

The Cuban Missile Crisis frightened the entire world. But how had the crisis arisen in the first place, and what were its consequences?

THE NUCLEAR THREAT

Nuclear weapons are the most destructive known to humankind, creating explosions many times more powerful than **conventional bombs.** These explosions also cause **radiation** that can kill people long after the blast. In 1945, near the end of World War II, the first **atomic bomb** flattened the Japanese city of Hiroshima, killing 80,000 people within seconds. The first nuclear weapons had to be dropped from airplanes. Then, in the 1950s, the Soviet Union built a rocket capable of traveling between continents—the ICBM, or Intercontinental Ballistic Missile. At the time of the Cuban Missile Crisis, the U.S. had many more weapons than the Soviets, but it did not have anything like an ICBM.

This U.S. short-range missile of 1957 could carry a nuclear warhead. Both the United States and the Soviet Union were rushing to build bigger and better weapons.

The Cold War

Mutual Assured Destruction

For 45 years, until the collapse of the **Soviet Union** in 1991, **communist** and non-communist countries viewed each other with suspicion. Military conflict was unlikely thanks to the theory of Mutual Assured Destruction, abbreviated as MAD. According to MAD, both **NATO** and the Warsaw Pact possessed enough nuclear weapons to effectively destroy human civilization. No matter which side began a nuclear war, the confrontation would turn the U.S., Europe, the USSR (the Soviet Union) and perhaps the whole globe into a pile of poisonous, radioactive rubble.

The arms race

For this reason the U.S. and the USSR avoided any armed conflict that could escalate into a nuclear war. But the two nations distrusted each other. The West

THE WORLD DIVIDED

When World War II ended in 1945, the world was split into two hostile camps. The U.S. and Western Europe believed that governments shouldn't interfere with daily business. The Soviet Union and Eastern Europe believed in communism, a system in which the government owns or controls industry and commerce. Each side feared the other and formed **alliances** for protection. In the East was the Warsaw Pact and in the West was the North Atlantic Treaty Organization (NATO).

This map from 1963 shows Europe divided into two hostile camps. On one side were the Warsaw Pact nations and on the other were the countries belonging to NATO.

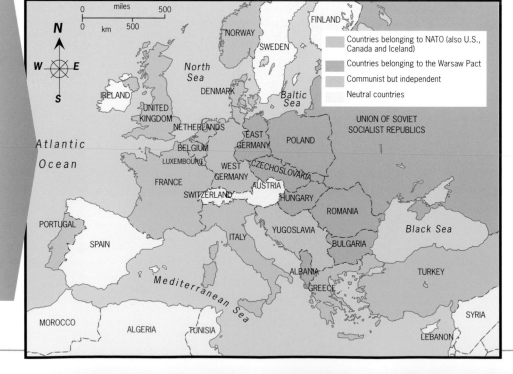

miles
0   500
0   500
km

Countries belonging to NATO (also U.S., Canada and Iceland)

Countries belonging to the Warsaw Pact

Communist but independent

Neutral countries

communism, and the Soviet Union feared that the West wanted to destroy it. Each side feared that if the other developed superior weapons, it might be tempted to attack despite MAD. Both sides spent huge amounts of money in a race to build better weapons. Meanwhile, **intelligence** agencies for both NATO and Warsaw Pact countries worked to discover what the other side was doing. Each side also tried to discredit the other in the eyes of the world. The era was known as the Cold War.

The Iron Curtain

The Cold War was most evident in Europe. The boundary between East and West was marked by heavily-guarded fences of barbed wire that ran along the borders of Yugoslavia, Hungary, East Germany, and Czechoslovakia. Berlin, the pre-war capital of Germany, was divided by a concrete wall patrolled day and night by communist troops. The Iron Curtain, as the frontier was called, was meant to keep enemies out of Eastern Europe, and also to keep citizens in. Many people did not like communism and wanted to escape to the West.

Built in 1961, the Berlin Wall was patrolled 24 hours a day by armed guards. It was meant to keep people from escaping from communist rule.

Europe was not the only place where the Cold War was fought. NATO and the Warsaw Pact nations each tried to win other countries over to their way of thinking. They supported wars and **revolutions** across the world, hoping that the winners would become their allies. So in 1959, when the communist leader Fidel Castro came to power in neighboring Cuba, it seemed like the United States' worst nightmare was about to come true.

Kennedy and Khrushchev

World leaders

In 1962, the world's most powerful men were U.S. President John F. Kennedy and Soviet Premier Nikita Khrushchev. When the Cuban Missile Crisis arose, it was up to them to solve it. They were two very different people who had to reach an agreement.

Kennedy and Khrushchev, the world's two most powerful men, smile happily at a meeting in Vienna in June 1961. A year later, their countries were almost at war.

Kennedy the anti-communist

Kennedy was born in 1917, the second oldest son in a wealthy family. Sworn in as president in 1961, he was, at the age of 44, the youngest president in the history of the U.S. He was strongly anti-**communist** and was particularly worried by the **Soviet Union's** nuclear **arsenal.** In 1961, the Soviet Union had sent the first manned spacecraft into orbit. The U.S. did not yet have such technology, and Kennedy knew that a rocket capable of carrying a person into space could just as well travel from one continent to another. Instead of a human cargo, it could be fitted with a nuclear warhead. To counteract this threat, Kennedy pumped money into developing his nation's rocket systems, while at the same time building more and more nuclear weapons.

THE "RED SCARE"

Many Americans were strongly opposed to communism. They were afraid that the "Reds," as communists were called, would take over the world. "I'd rather be dead than Red" was one popular saying, as was "There's a Red under every bed." Between 1950 and 1954, a politician named Joseph McCarthy launched a harsh campaign against citizens suspected of being communists. Many innocent people's careers or lives were ruined as a result of these investigations. Many other Western nations were also frightened by the "Red Scare."

The same rockets that put the Soviet Union's *Sputnik* space satellite into orbit in 1957 could also carry nuclear warheads between continents.

The balance of power

Nikita Khrushchev was a miner's son, born in 1894. He had worked as a shepherd and as a locksmith before entering politics. When he came to power in 1958, he was 62 years old. Unlike Soviet rulers before him, he had no wish to destroy the West. Rather, he wanted communist states to live peacefully alongside those with open economies. He was worried, however, that the United States had more nuclear weapons than the Soviets. He feared that if the United States got too far ahead in the arms race it might be tempted to attack, even though the Soviets had better rockets. He was also worried by the presence of U.S. missiles in Turkey, right on the Soviet border. In order to restore the balance of power he, like Kennedy, ordered more weapons to be built. At the same time he searched for a base from which he could threaten the United States. When Fidel Castro seized power in Cuba in 1959, Khrushchev saw a perfect opportunity.

Cuba and Castro

Slavery and sugar

Cuba's history is a troubled one. In 1492, Christopher Columbus claimed the island as a Spanish **colony.** For more than 300 years, African slaves were shipped to Cuba where they worked, in terrible conditions, to grow and harvest tobacco, timber, and sugar. Spanish landowners, who paid their slaves nothing, grew wealthier. Slavery was not abolished in Cuba until 1886. By then, the majority of the population were of African or mixed descent.

The fight for independence

In 1895, Cuban revolutionaries started a war for independence, which they won in 1898 with help from the U.S. But although Cuba may have freed itself from Spain, it now found itself little more than a U.S. colony. In theory it was a **democracy,** where everyone had a vote. But, due to requirements set by the United States, the vote was denied to Africans, women, and those who owned less than $250. This excluded all but a few people. For more than 50 years, Cuba was ruled by various corrupt **puppet governments.** In 1952, a **dictator** named General Fulgencio Batista—who was backed by the U.S. government—blatantly seized power. His regime was a corrupt and cruel one. As opposition to him grew, many thousands were murdered and many more were imprisoned.

President Batista greets supporters in 1955. Batista's regime became corrupt, and most Cubans grew to dislike him.

By this time, U.S. companies controlled many Cuban businesses. The U.S. government owned large areas of Cuban land and had a naval base at the port of Guantánamo. U.S. involvement brought much-needed money to Cuba, but many Cubans disliked being controlled by a foreign power. There already had been several rebellions against U.S. influence. In 1953, a new **revolution** began. Its leader was Fidel Castro.

Castro the revolutionary

Born in 1926, Castro had graduated from law school in 1950 with a burning desire to reform Cuban politics and to free the island from U.S. control. He was a **socialist,** favoring tight government control of industry and the marketplace. He tried to implement change by running for office, but when Batista put an end to democratic elections, this was no longer possible. Castro took to the hills and for six years waged a **guerrilla war** against Batista. He was aided by the Argentinian **communist** revolutionary Che Guevara, who played an important part in the Cuban revolution. Batista's government collapsed in 1959, leaving Castro in control of the island.

Castro poses with two armed supporters in 1957. Between 1953 and 1959, he waged a guerrilla war against the Batista government.

CASTRO'S WAR

Castro was supported by most Cuban peasants. Non-Cubans owned 75% of Cuba's farmland. Five U.S. sugar companies alone controlled two million acres. Cuba's oil refineries and its electricity company were foreign-owned. It is no wonder that many Cubans wanted a new government. Yet Cuba's more prosperous professionals saw Castro as a menace. Thousands fled with their families to Florida, hoping one day to return to their homeland.

Bay of Pigs

Castro upsets the United States

Although many Americans supported Cuba's **revolution** at first, the tide of public opinion in the U.S. rapidly turned against Castro. One of the first acts of the new revolutionary government was to **nationalize** foreign assets and to pass laws restricting the amount of land individuals could own. Americans were outraged as U.S. firms were stripped of their Cuban assets. In retaliation, the U.S. refused to buy Cuban sugar and stopped trade in all but the most basic items such as food and medicine.

Castro's response was to turn to **communist** countries such as the **Soviet Union.** As a result, the USSR became Cuba's main trading partner, providing considerable economic as well as military aid. This angered the U.S. further, and the government decided that Castro had to be overthrown at all costs. To achieve this, the U.S. plotted with Cuban **exiles** to make a full-scale invasion. Throughout 1960, the **CIA** trained exiles for an invasion of Cuba.

Protesters in the United States march against Castro in April 1961. He was unpopular in the U.S. because he was a communist and had taken property in Cuba away from American people.

The invasion fiasco

On April 17, 1961, five merchant ships that had been leased by the CIA put ashore 1,300 Cuban exiles in the *Bahia de Cochinos,* or "Bay of Pigs." Their plan was to march inland, gathering support as they went, and seize control of the island. It was a disaster. The men landed, but as the invaders moved inland they found that nobody wanted to join them. They had expected military assistance from the U.S., but

President Kennedy decided against open support. On April 19, after just 72 hours, the invasion came to a humiliating end. Castro claimed outright victory, having taken more than 1,000 prisoners of war.

Castro seeks a reconciliation

Remarkably, after this act of aggression, Castro urged the U.S. to reestablish friendly relations. There was no reason, he argued, why the two countries could not exist as neighbors. The U.S., however, did not wish to have a communist country so close to its borders. It secretly began a new wave of **sabotage** and **assassinations.** *"Communist domination in this hemisphere can never be negotiated,"* President Kennedy told the world.

Prisoners of war line up after the Bay of Pigs disaster. Almost all of the 1,300 invaders were captured by Castro's army. Many were exiles hoping to regain property they had lost when Castro came to power. Most were released when the crisis was over. The last one was let out in 1986.

THE MONROE DOCTRINE

The United States resists foreign interference in either North or South America. This policy is known as the Monroe Doctrine. Dating back to 1823, it states:

"The American continents, by the free and independent condition which they have assumed and maintain, are henceforth not to be considered as subjects for the future colonization by any European powers. . . .

We owe it therefore to the candor and to the amicable relations existing between the United States and those [European] powers to declare that we should consider any attempt on their part to extend their system to any portion of this hemisphere as dangerous to our peace and safety."

Buildup

The new regime

Ordinary people in Castro's Cuba were doing well. More people than ever before could read and write. A nationwide campaign against dangerous diseases such as diphtheria, tetanus, and whooping cough had made the population healthier. Everybody was better educated and, thanks to the new rules governing land ownership, everyone had a chance to work their own farms. All that was keeping Cuba from succeeding as Castro wanted it to was the United States trade **embargo**—and the threat of invasion.

Castro had every reason to fear an invasion by U.S. forces. He appealed to the United Nations, but the majority of its members chose to support the United States. He therefore had little choice but to look to the USSR for help. Nikita Khrushchev was only too pleased to be of assistance.

Photographs from U.S. spy planes showed exactly what the Soviets were doing in Cuba. They picked out the launch sites and could even identify the type of missiles being used.

CHERRY PICKER
LAUNCH PAD WITH ERECTOR
LAUNCH PAD WITH ERECTOR
MISSILE READY BLDGS
OXIDIZER VEHICLES
FUELING VEHICLES

Spying on Cuba

Khrushchev was happy to help Castro for political reasons. He was pleased that Cuba was on its way to becoming a **communist** state along Soviet lines. But he also had Soviet military needs in mind. **NATO** had **nuclear missiles** in Turkey, about 160 miles (257 kilometers) from Soviet territory. In Khrushchev's view, Cuba was the perfect opportunity for getting even.

Soviet ships slipped quietly into Cuban ports with troops and equipment. U.S. spy planes were a constant hazard, so soldiers dressed as tourists to avoid detection. In their holds, the ships contained everything that was needed for a nuclear strike against the U.S.

On August 29, 1962, an American U-2 spy plane photographed something unusual. It looked like a missile site. On October 15, as further photographs came in, it became obvious that nuclear weapons were being set up on Cuban soil. The clock had started ticking.

SPIES AND SPYING

Both the United States and the **Soviet Union** used spies to monitor the activities of one another. The U.S. had the advantage in the air, because its high-level U-2 planes could take photographs without risking attack by Soviet fighters. In Europe, spies from each country used mini-cameras and listening devices to track each other. Some used concealed gas-guns and poison-darts to kill enemy agents.

President Kennedy meets the Soviet ambassador and foreign minister (plus an interpreter) in October 1962. The Soviets denied that there were any missiles in Cuba.

A Threat to the U.S.

Generals tell Kennedy to invade

The U.S. panicked at the thought of Soviet missiles so close to its border. Kennedy felt particularly badly betrayed because the Soviets had told him, through secret channels, that they would never put missiles in Cuba. On October 16, he summoned a group of advisers known as EX-COMM, or the Executive Committee of the United States National Security Council. Some, including President Kennedy's brother Bobby, wanted to settle the matter by peaceful discussion. Others, mostly generals, favored an immediate air strike, followed by an invasion. Plans for an invasion were already in place. It was code-named "Operation Mongoose."

For the next few days, Kennedy kept to his usual schedule, as if nothing had happened. It was important to keep the matter secret because if the public knew what was going on there might be a national panic. Another worry was that if the Soviets knew that the U.S. government was aware of what was happening in Cuba, they might fire the missiles to prevent an invasion.

President Kennedy is shown here with his brother Bobby. Bobby Kennedy was a useful negotiator with the Soviet ambassador in Washington during the Missile Crisis.

Blockade or invasion?

Finally, EX-COMM came up with two approaches to the situation. The first was invasion. The second was a "quarantine," or naval blockade, which would keep military supplies from reaching Cuba. EX-COMM warned Kennedy that Khrushchev would respond angrily to either option. On October 21, spy planes photographed bombers and Soviet MiG fighter planes being assembled in northern Cuba.

Kennedy chose the quarantine. He called it this because a blockade was an act of war under international law. Kennedy reasoned that this would give the Soviets time to think things over. At 7:00 P.M. on October 22, 1962, he spoke to the nation on television about his decision. For seventeen minutes, the nation watched anxiously as their president told of the danger that threatened them and of the action he intended to take in their defense. In case Khrushchev wanted to fight, U.S. missiles were put on standby.

This shows Cuba at the time of the Missile Crisis.

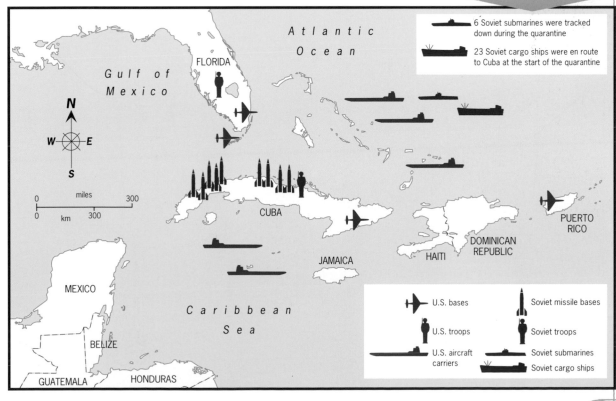

6 Soviet submarines were tracked down during the quarantine

23 Soviet cargo ships were en route to Cuba at the start of the quarantine

Atlantic Ocean

FLORIDA

Gulf of Mexico

N
W — E
S

miles
0   300
0   300
km

CUBA

PUERTO RICO

DOMINICAN REPUBLIC

JAMAICA   HAITI

MEXICO

Caribbean Sea

BELIZE

GUATEMALA   HONDURAS

U.S. bases

U.S. troops

U.S. aircraft carriers

Soviet missile bases

Soviet troops

Soviet submarines

Soviet cargo ships

The Quarantine

Armies on standby

The quarantine came too late. There were at least twenty Soviet nuclear warheads on Cuban soil, as well as tens of thousands of Soviet troops. Castro's own army was on standby for action, and an additional twenty warheads were on their way.

Londoners protested against the Cuban Missile Crisis. It was feared that the events in Cuba would cause another world war.

Khrushchev was shaken by Kennedy's speech. Never imagining that the U.S. would go to war over Cuba, he had simply ordered his ships to proceed to Havana, Cuba's capital. But now there were about 300 U.S. Navy warships heading for Cuba, with orders to stop and search any vessel that approached the island. If necessary, they could open fire.

Two days after Kennedy's announcement, Castro wrote to Khrushchev that under no circumstances should the U.S. be allowed to fire the first nuclear weapon in the event of an invasion. Khrushchev warned Kennedy that the missiles were there solely for defensive purposes and that any invasion would present *"a serious threat to the peace and security of peoples,"*—by which he meant war. *"You have thrown down the gauntlet,"* he declared.

Eyeball to eyeball

Khrushchev, however, did tell his captains not to fight. The quarantine started at 10:00 A.M. on October 24. The first Soviet ships were drawing near and the U.S. feared it would have to open fire. Because communications were so slow, they had no way of knowing whether the ships' captains had received any orders from their superiors in Moscow. To make matters worse, the ships were being shadowed by Soviet nuclear submarines. But finally, at 10:25 A.M., the Soviet ships turned back.

Open conflict had been avoided, but it was a close call. *"We were eyeball to eyeball,"* said U.S. Secretary of State Dean Rusk, *"and the other guy just blinked."*

Soviet nuclear submarines shadowed Soviet freighters heading for Cuba. Their presence made the crisis even more explosive.

Trouble in the Air

Full alert

The nightmare was not over yet. With thousands of Soviet military personnel and at least twenty **nuclear missiles** still on Cuban soil, some U.S. forces had been placed on DEFCON 2, the highest state of military alert yet reached. They could attack Cuba or the **Soviet Union** at a moment's notice.

The Americans had good cause to be worried. By this time, spy planes were flying over Cuba twice a day at heights of only 350 feet. On the same day that U.S. forces were put on full alert, one pilot reported that a missile was being tested for launching. As he said, *"When you can almost see the writing on the side of the missiles then you really know what you've got."*

U-2 spy planes such as this first spotted the Soviets building missiles in Cuba. Low-level "Crusader" jets later provided more detailed photographs.

A compromise

At the beginning of the crisis, Khrushchev had tried to bluff as though he would attack, thinking that the U.S. would not risk war over Cuba. But once the Soviet ships were forced to turn back, he knew the bluff wasn't working. On October 26, he offered to remove the **nuclear missiles** from Cuba if the U.S. promised not to invade.

Spy plane shot down

There was more tension on October 27, when a U.S. spy plane was shot down by a Soviet ground-to-air missile and its pilot was killed. Afterward, U.S. spy planes were greeted by a hail of rifle fire and anti-aircraft shells fired by jittery Cuban soldiers. Another plane was damaged, but the pilot was able to make his way home.

Moscow claimed that the officer who had fired the ground-to-air missile had acted without orders. This showed how dangerous the situation was—if Soviet commanders in Cuba could do what they wanted, then no amount of high-level **diplomacy** would solve the crisis.

Cuban soldiers are shown here operating an anti-aircraft gun. Even with out-dated equipment, Cuban forces brought down several U.S. planes.

Another narrow escape

That same day, another American pilot narrowly escaped death. He had taken off from Alaska and had accidentally flown over Soviet territory. As soon as his plane was detected by **radar,** Soviet fighters were sent after it. The man realized his mistake and changed course for Alaska just before the fighters caught up with him. U.S. bombers were ready to **retaliate** if the plane was shot down. It was a close call.

The incident put both sides' air forces on full alert. Their planes were armed with nuclear bombs. The world teetered on the edge of a catastrophic war.

Escalation

Khrushchev raises the stakes

When the spy plane was shot down over Cuban territory, Kennedy was still considering Khrushchev's offer to remove the missiles in return for a promise not to invade Cuba. Now, Khrushchev felt his position was stronger. In a second message, he demanded that the U.S. also remove its missiles from Turkey.

The pilot was killed when this U.S. spy plane was shot down over Cuba.

World peace threatened

Many had hoped that the crisis in Cuba could be resolved locally. But now it was linked to the Cold War struggle in Europe. If the U.S. removed its missiles from Turkey, it might undermine **NATO's** standing. A peaceful solution seemed unlikely.

SLOW COMMUNICATIONS

During the crisis, Khrushchev and Kennedy chose to write letters to one another rather than sending coded messages by telephone. At a time when a single correspondence could mean the difference between peace and war, it could take five to six hours for Khrushchev to receive a letter from Kennedy. This delay was a matter of concern for the leadership of both countries, but it was equally important for the leaders to be able to choose their words thoughtfully and carefully.

One way out would have been to discuss matters at the United Nations. But that had already proved useless. Despite Castro's objections, many nations approved of the action the U.S. was taking. When asked about their missiles at a UN conference on October 25, the Soviets simply refused to answer.

Something had to be done—and fast. There was always the danger that Soviet commanders in Cuba might take matters into their own hands. Without orders from Moscow, they could fire their **nuclear missiles** with the same ease as they had shot down the U.S. spy plane. As the minutes ticked by, the world held its breath.

Cuba protested at the United Nations, but the UN chose not to restrict U.S. interference in Cuban affairs. U.S. actions were approved by a vote of 50 to 11—with 39 countries refusing to vote.

The Solution

A way out

The United States chose the simplest way out. Ignoring Khrushchev's second letter, Kennedy replied to the first. He agreed not to invade Cuba if the Soviets withdrew their men and their missiles. Speed was now so important that he did not bother with letters but broadcast his decision on public radio, which the Soviets were bound to pick up.

President Kennedy inspects his men and equipment. At the height of the crisis, U.S. missiles were on constant standby.

In case this did not work, Kennedy drew up plans to remove the U.S. missiles from Turkey. What he never admitted to the **Soviet Union** was that these missiles were old and due to be removed anyway.

All they could do now was hope that Khrushchev accepted. *"It was a hope, not an expectation,"* Bobby Kennedy explained. In fact, his expectation was that the two sides would be at war the next day.

Agreement

On October 28, Khrushchev agreed to the terms, and like Kennedy he announced his decision on the radio. Some U.S. generals thought it was a trick to buy time and suggested bombing Cuba anyway. Luckily, Kennedy realized Khrushchev's message was sincere and quickly broadcast his acceptance. After fourteen terrifying days, the crisis was over.

But it was not until November 21, that Kennedy finally lowered the alert from DEFCON 2 to DEFCON 4. This was after the Soviet missiles had been shipped out of Cuba, carefully stacked on deck so that U.S. pilots could count them from the air, and the Soviet bombers were being **dismantled.**

EXTRACT FROM KENNEDY'S LETTER TO KHRUSHCHEV

"I have read your letter of October 26th with great care and welcomed the statement of your desire to seek a prompt solution to the problem. The first thing that needs to be done, however, is for work to cease on offensive missile bases in Cuba....

I would like to say again that the United States is very much interested in reducing tensions and halting the arms race...."

A U.S. Navy vessel steams alongside a Soviet freighter leaving Cuba. The dismantled missiles are clearly visible on the ship's deck.

What If?

Invasion

What if Khrushchev had not backed down? In that case, the United States would have had no choice but to invade. Its plans had already been worked out. U.S. **intelligence** estimated that there were 10,000 Soviet troops on Cuba and perhaps 100,000 men under Castro's control. The U.S. therefore planned to fly 1,080 air strikes to weaken Cuban defenses for an **amphibious invasion** by 180,000 soldiers.

Had the U.S. gone ahead, it would have had a nasty surprise. The Soviets actually had over 40,000 men in Cuba. In addition, Castro's army numbered 270,000 instead of 100,000. On top of this, there were the Soviet **nuclear missiles.** The United States assumed they were all long-range. In fact, a number of them were for short-range battlefield use and commanders had been authorized to use them without permission from Moscow.

During the 1960s, the threat of nuclear war hung over the world. In the 1965 film *Dr. Strangelove*, actor Peter Sellers (right) played a U.S. president trying to stop the bombing of Russia by order of a paranoid air force commander.

A world disaster

An invasion would have been a disaster. The fighting would have been brutal. The United States would have had to send in more troops and more planes. The Cubans and Soviets would have been left with no choice but to use their nuclear weapons.

Once the first nuclear missile had been launched, the United States would have **retaliated** by using its own nuclear weapons, not in Cuba where American troops would be, but against the USSR. The Soviets would have responded by launching their own missiles against the U.S. This would have led to the very situation both sides hoped to avoid—MAD, Mutual Assured Destruction.

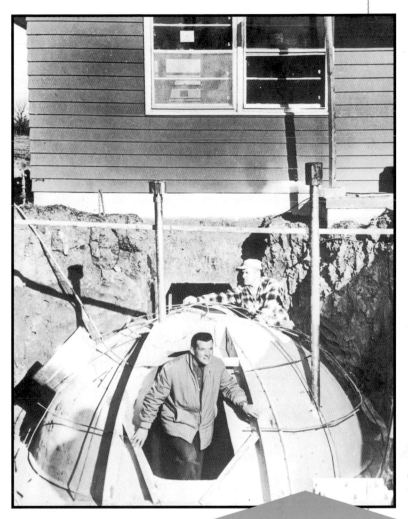

CASTRO LOSES OUT

Castro felt betrayed by Khrushchev's decision. He tried unsuccessfully to halt the removal of missiles and insisted that the United States accept a number of other conditions. The U.S. government refused. Among the conditions were the following:

- an end to the trade **embargo** against Cuba
- an end to undercover **sabotage** operations
- an end to reconnaissance missions in Cuban air and sea space
- the evacuation of the U.S. naval base in Guantánamo

Throughout the U.S., people dreaded a nuclear attack. Some families added bomb shelters to their homes, hoping to survive if the Soviet missiles were actually launched.

Back from the Brink

Kennedy's assassination

Kennedy and Khrushchev, the world's two most powerful leaders, had the closest relationship of any U.S. and Soviet leaders since the Cold War started. But neither remained in power long enough to develop the relationship. Kennedy was **assassinated** in November 1963, and in 1964, Khrushchev was forced out of office by politicians who saw his compromise over Cuba as a dangerous sign of weakness. Castro, meanwhile, was left fuming. Although the crisis was over, the U.S. still refused to trade with Cuba, leaving it an impoverished island dependent on an weakened **Soviet Union.**

The Hotline

But something had been learned. According to one of Kennedy's advisers, *"Having come so close to the edge, we must make it our business not to pass this way again."* Nine months after the end of the Cuban Missile Crisis, the U.S. and the Soviet Union agreed to stop testing nuclear weapons in the atmosphere. They also saw how risky slow communications could

Many people opposed the arms race caused by the Cold War. Here anti-nuclear protesters gather in London's Trafalgar Square.

be. At the height of the crisis, if either Kennedy or Khrushchev had responded by letter instead of broadcasting over public radio, the delay might have been disastrous. As a result, the two superpowers installed a telephone hotline in August 1963 so that their leaders could discuss problems before they reached a dangerous level.

Both sides continued to distrust each other. Each side feared that the other might gain an advantage, and so the nuclear arms race continued. But the events in Cuba had taught them the need for caution. It was the nearest the world has ever come to destruction. Although there have been other crises since, none has been as potentially devastating as the Cuban Missile Crisis.

Ronald Reagan and Mikhail Gorbachev signed an anti-nuclear treaty in December 1987. This was a major step toward ending the arms race.

END OF THE COLD WAR

The Soviet Union collapsed in 1991. By that time, however, it had made several important agreements with the U.S. aimed at stopping the arms race. Among them were the Strategic Arms Limitation Talks (SALT) of 1969 and 1972. Then, in 1987, U.S. President Ronald Reagan and Mikhail Gorbachev of the Soviet Union signed an agreement to reduce their stockpiles of nuclear weapons. This led to the Strategic Arms Reduction Talks (START) of 1990. Over the next decade, the Cold War came to an end. Both sides destroyed hundreds of **nuclear missiles,** but many remain.

Important Dates

1959	January 1	Fidel Castro seizes power in Cuba
1960	December 19	Castro declares Cuba's support for the **Soviet Union**
1961	January 3	The United States cuts diplomatic relations with Cuba
	April 12	Kennedy promises not to use force to overthrow Castro
	April 17	A group of Cuban **exiles,** backed by the U.S., invades Cuba at the Bay of Pigs. They are defeated in three days.
1962	July 27	Castro announces that he has invited the Soviet Union to help defend Cuba
	August 29	U.S. spy planes identify signs of military activity in Cuba
	October 15	U.S. spy planes confirm that missile sites are being built in Cuba
	October 17	Kennedy's advisers press for an air strike against Cuba
	October 22	Kennedy tells Americans of the Cuban situation and announces a "quarantine," (naval blockade) to prevent military supplies from reaching Cuba
	October 22	Khrushchev calls the U.S. action *"a serious threat to the peace and security of peoples"*
	October 24	The U.S. quarantine takes effect. Soviet ships turn back at the last moment. U.S. forces go to DEFCON 2.
	October 26	U.S. spy planes show that work at the missile sites in Cuba has increased. Khrushchev announces he will remove the weapons if the U.S. promises not to invade Cuba.
	October 27	A U.S. spy plane is shot down over Cuba. Khrushchev raises the stakes by saying he will remove the missiles only if the U.S. removes its own missiles based in Turkey.
	October 28	Kennedy ignores the new ultimatum and agrees to Khrushchev's first proposal. Khrushchev announces he will remove the missiles on the understanding that the U.S. will not invade Cuba.
	November 21	All missiles having been removed from Cuba, Soviet bombers are **dismantled** and shipped home. The crisis is over at last.

Glossary

alliance two or more countries grouped together for a common cause

amphibious invasion attack in which ships are used to land troops ashore

arsenal store of weapons

assassinate to murder someone deliberately for political reasons

atomic bomb extremely powerful weapon powered by uranium and plutonium. A single A-bomb can flatten a city.

CIA (Central Intelligence Agency) U.S. government agency set up to gather information about potential threats to national security

colony territory belonging to another country

communism social, political, and economic society in which private ownership is banned and everything is controlled by the state. A person who believes in communism is a communist.

conventional bomb bomb that is not powered by uranium or plutonium

democracy society run by its citizens, who vote to elect leaders and pass laws

dictator ruler of a country who has absolute power

diplomacy skillful and tactful negotiations, often with people from foreign governments

dismantle to take something apart

embargo order that stops trade with another country

exile someone who has been forced to live outside his or her home country, often for political reasons

guerrilla war war between a traditional army and a smaller, less well-equipped force that uses hit-and-run tactics

intelligence secret information gathered by spies and by other means that tells one nation what another is doing

nationalize to take a business out of private ownership and make it public property

NATO (North Atlantic Treaty Organization) defensive alliance formed between democratic countries of Europe and North America in order to curb Soviet aggression in Europe

nuclear missile rocket that has an atomic warhead

puppet government government that is manipulated by another country

radar system that uses radio waves to detect objects at long range

radiation invisible, deadly rays that are produced in a nuclear explosion. Materials that emit radiation are said to be radioactive.

retaliate to attack an enemy that has struck first

revolution overthrow of a government by force

sabotage secret destruction of buildings and machinery

socialist someone who believes that government should control the economy to ensure that everyone is treated fairly

Soviet Union a group of communist countries headed by Russia. Its capital was Moscow.

More Books to Read

Kent, Zachary. *John F. Kennedy*. Danbury, Conn.: Children's Press, 1987.

Morrison, Marion. *Cuba*. Danbury, Conn.: Children's Press, 1999.

Press, Petra. *Fidel Castro*. Chicago: Heinemann Library, 2000.

Index